W9-CGY-508

HOTDOGGING
AND
SNOWBOARDING

THE NYACK LIBRARY
NYACK, N. Y. 10960

PUBLISHED BY
Capstone Press
Mankato, Minnesota USA

CIP
LIBRARY OF CONGRESS CATALOGING IN PUBLICATION DATA

Guthrie, Robert W.
 Hot dogging and snow boarding / by Robert W. Guthrie
   p. cm. — (Action sports)
 Summary: Introduces the relatively new sports of freestyle skiing and snowboarding.

 ISBN 1-56065-052-4:
 1. Ski acrobatics—juvenile literature. 2. Snow boarding—juvenile literature. [1. Ski acrobatics. 2. Snowboarding.]
 I. Title. II. Series.
 GV854.9.A25G88 1989
 796.93'7-dc20   89-27873
                  CIP
                  AC

Photo Credits

Linda Waidhofer: 4, 7
Brian W. Robb: 12, 14, 15, 16, 17, 19, 20, 25, 27, 28, 32, 33, 37, 38
World Wide Ski Corporation: 22, 23, 43
Stephen C. Datnoff: 24, 31

by Robert W. Guthrie
1942-1991

This book is dedicated to all young readers by the parents of Robert Guthrie with the hope that they will enjoy the book as much as the sport of skiing. Bob Guthrie loved the sport and wanted to share his love with young readers.

Copyright ©1992 by Capstone Press, Inc. All rights reserved. No part of this book may be reproduced in any form without written permission from the publisher, except for brief passages included in a review. Printed in the United States of America.

Capstone Press
P.O. Box 669, Mankato, MN, U.S.A. 56002-0669

CONTENTS

Telluride, Colorado's movie star dog, Zudnik.

IN THE BEGINNING

You are sitting in a chairlift thirty feet above the ground. A cable pulls you and your instructor up the mountain. As you brush by the tops of snow-covered pine trees, you anxiously watch skiers crisscrossing the slopes below. A cold breeze brushes across your face. You feel a bit dizzy. You peer nervously down the mountain. You wonder if this is a good idea. Slide down a massive mountain on two strips of fiberglass called skis? It seemed like fun at the bottom. Everyone you know who skis likes it.

You cling tightly to the chair's post and watch the skiers. You focus on other beginners like yourself. They move slowly, stiffly, and some fall. Again, you wonder about this idea of going back down the slope on skis. You can see the more advanced skiers move like dandelion puffs floating on air. They appear graceful, and the only sound they make is the swish of their skis.

Through a break in the trees, you see someone moving like a surfer down the slope. He rides on something resembling a narrow surfboard. As he gets closer, you see the swirls of color on his board.

The rider approaches a bump, hits it, and flies into the air, shouting, "Yahoo!" In a spray of snow, he lands hard and turns fast. He laughs. The "surfer" is snowboarding.

Another advanced skier barrels down the slope. As she approaches a crest, she pushes her poles in the ground. Suddenly she does a somersault in the air. Landing beautifully, she continues down the hill a short way, then performs a few more spins before she is out of sight. Her gymnastics are part of a special sport called freestyle skiing, once called **hotdogging.** Freestyle skiing is for people who really know what they are doing. Hotdogging is a thing of the past.

Now it's your turn, and you know that it will demand your total concentration to make it down the slope. Suddenly you realize that, just as your instructor explained at the beginning, this is not a sport that everyone loves. But now, you are in control and your determination and concentration take you down the mountain.

Whew! You know that it was not an Olympic run, but you also know that you will continue to learn this sport. Each time you ski you will improve your techniques and fundamentals.

Kristin Taylor of the U.S. Freestyle Team

HISTORY OF FREESTYLE SKIING

Freestyle skiing is a magical combination of skiing, skating, dancing, and gymnastics. It was very popular during the '70s.

How did this sport get started? Many freestyle skiers have discovered that freestyle is a way to express their own individual abilities and talents. Also, many freestyle skiers became interested in freestyle when they were bored with running **gates**—skiing the curved routes past the little flags in **slalom skiing.**

In 1929, a European skier named Dr. Fritz Reuel tried some spins and **pole flips.** He then helped other skiers learn tricks on skis.

In the 1950s, a top skier from Norway, Stein Erickson, added something new. He started to do flying leaps on skis. He even did upside-down leaps. He inspired other skiers to try them and invent their own tricks. They did **back scratchers,** with the backs of their skis almost touching their backs. They did **helicopters,** spinning two or three times in the air, and many others.

In the 1960s, some American skiers decided to name this new sport. They called it hot dog skiing or hotdogging. They called themselves hotdoggers. Like the hippies of the 1960s, they often had long hair and wild clothes.

They were daredevils on the slopes and attracted huge crowds.

American hotdoggers soon decided they should compete with each other. They also wanted to show their tricks off. In 1966, some of the best hotdoggers started performing for the public. They tried to outdo each other. They invented new ways to spin and fly through the air on skis.

Early in 1971, the first major "hot dog" contest was held. The K-2 Hot Dog contest was open to everyone. Hotdoggers from all over the West came to the ski resort in Aspen, Colorado. Many skied fast and did dangerous tricks, such as backward helicopters. Other skiers were slower and more graceful. And some hotdoggers were hilarious. One of them, Bob "Boogie" Mann, became famous for sitting back on his skis and spinning very slowly. He had invented the **slow dog noodle.**

Many skiers wanted the sport to become more serious. Soon they dropped the "hotdogging" name and image and replaced it with "freestyle skiing." They thought it should have clear rules and goals. In April 1971, the North American Freestyle Championships were held in Vail, Colorado. The event was divided into three completely separate parts and the competition was held on three different ski runs. One run had five jumps. It tested the contestants' skills in **aerial skiing**. In this event, the skiers tried flying leaps and flips. Another run was rather flat. This one tested skills in **ballet skiing.**

The skiers did slow spins, leaps, and pole flips. The third run was a very steep, bumpy hill called "Look Ma." It challenged the experts in **mogul skiing.** In skiing the moguls (bumps), the skiers used aerial and ballet skills. They tried to ski fast and gracefully through the huge moguls.

Some contestants tried to do well in all three, competing to be the overall champion. Scotty Brooksbank stayed at or near the top of the overall standings for seven years. Other freestylers tried to excel in just one of the three. A few, like Wayne Wong and Suzy Chaffee, became famous for their ballet tricks. Wong was a master of all the moves. He invented an amazing flip called the **Wong Banger.** It was a shoulder roll in the air, followed by a handspring. Chaffee also brought music to freestyle skiing.

After that grand beginning in 1971, freestyle skiing grew steadily. Some contests offered more than $100,000 in prize money. The money and excitement led to many new tricks, including triple flips. Many people were doing tricks just for fun. In 1975, nineteen skiers at Grand Targhee Ski Resort in Wyoming held hands and did a back flip at the same time.

All this excitement eventually led to some serious injuries in the mogul and aerial events. A few skiers became paralyzed in accidents caused by crashing while doing **inverted** (upside-down) **jumps**. For several years Americans had to go to Europe to compete in freestyle skiing. Meanwhile, American coaches began to work to make aerial skiing a safer sport.

In 1988, freestyle skiing was included as a "demonstration sport" in the Winter Olympics in Calgary, Canada. This meant the sport was being tested for future Olympics. It passed the test and was an official sport in the 1992 Winter Olympics.

The U.S. Freestyle Ski Team worked hard to prepare for the 1992 Olympics. U.S. freestylers wanted to show what they could do in this colorful, exciting event.

In March of 1992, over 7,200 junior freestyle skiers competed in the 13- to 18-year-old category. This included slalom, giant slalom, downhill, and super G slots at six different ski areas in the U.S.

Today's freestylers are no longer the "hotdoggers" of the '70s. Special training is available for anyone interested in this exciting action sport.

Andrew Ivanov skiing moguls during 1992 Olympics in Albertville, France

WAYS TO BE A FREESTYLE SKIER

Freestyling has three main areas: moguls, ballet, and aerials. One of these three areas is not too difficult if you are a good skier. The other two take a lot of special training and practice.

Mogul Skiing

Mogul skiing is the easiest kind of freestyle. Moguls are on any well-used ski slope. Moguls are hills of snow packed down by skiers passing over the same spot. Mogul skiing is a lot like regular downhill skiing, except that mogul skiers have to plan a course between the bumps. It is hard to jump in the bumps without a "crash landing."

Mogul skiers also try three types of stunts. One stunt is skiing through the moguls with perfect form. Another stunt is going as fast as they can without losing control. The third stunt is the jump. The easiest jump is the **pop.** There is also the **spread eagle,** the helicopter, and the **zudnik.**

Jumping in the bumps is the most exciting part of mogul skiing. It is also the most difficult and dangerous. Even good skiers must have good instruction and practice a lot. The landing is the hardest part of all. If mogul skiers do not absorb the shock, they will collapse in a tangle of arms, legs, and skis.

Ballet Skiing

At first, ballet skiing is harder than moguls for most skiers. Skiers must make moves they are not used to making, unless they are skaters or dancers, or do spins and jumps all the time.

Even if they have learned skating or dancing, they still must be good skiers. Also, they still have to learn what moves are right for skiing. The three basic moves are spins, jumps, and flips.

Ballet is hard to learn without careful training. There are also some strict rules to follow.

Coaches demonstrating flips at the Freestyle International Summer Ski Camp

Ballet training at Summer Ski Camp on Mt. Hood, Oregon

Student practices on the water ramp at the Freestyle International Summer Ski Camp

Aerial Skiing

Aerial skiing takes a lot of special practice. Skiers cannot be sloppy when they do the hard leaps.

Freestyle ski coaches work hard on safety. They take aerial skiers through a step-by-step training program. Skiers first work with a coach by tumbling on a mat. Then they practice jumping on the trampoline. Next they train on a diving board. Coaches make the skiers practice the right moves hundreds of times before they try it on skis.

Even if you are not advanced enough to do flips, you can do many exciting jumps. If you have the ability and train hard enough, you can become a real aerial skier. You can be a skier in the sky.

Christian Risavec skiing aerials during 1992 Olympics in Albertville, France

THE HISTORY OF SNOWBOARDING

If you like skateboarding or surfing in the summer, snowboarding may be the winter action sport for you.

In the mid 1960s, a small piece of plywood shaped like a surfboard appeared on the ski slopes. It had a rope on one end, like a sled does, and was called a **Snurfer.** It was very hard to control. Two men, Jake Carpenter of Vermont and Tom Sims of California, decided they wanted to make a better board.

Carpenter and Sims finally designed a board that looked like a single water ski. It had straps in a sideways position to hold the feet. The rider stood on it as a surfer does, and did not wear ski boots. Good winter boots allowed the straps to be adjusted to fit.

During the 1981-82 ski season, the first big snowboarding contest was held in Colorado. The best snowboarders competed in the King of the Mountain Snowboard Championships. Next was the National Championship of Snowboarding in Vermont. At first, ski slope owners were afraid that the boards were unsafe. Also, people thought snowboarders were kind of strange. They looked a lot like the freestyle "hotdoggers" of the late 1960s and early 1970s.

Snowboard action on Mt. Hood, Oregon

Deep powder snowboarding at Mt. Hood Meadows, Oregon

In 1985, a few well-known U.S. ski areas made a change. They required skill tests or lessons. Now the door was finally open. Soon, the snowboarders were on the slopes.

In the last few years, more and more ski slopes have opened up to snowboarders. Now most areas allow them, and there are more than 300,000 snowboarders in the U.S.

Many things make snowboarders different from skiers. Their outfits and equipment come in very bright surfing colors, and they have their own language. The sport is called **shredding,** and sometimes snowboarders call themselves **shredheads.** Some of them call their boards **shred sleds.** One of their biggest thrills is getting **big air,** which is a very high jump. If they go even higher, they get **monster air.** If their knees are too far apart, they are doing the **stinkbug.** If they take a really bad fall, they are **road pizza.**

Snowboard contests have increased. The best boarders compete in four events, the **downhill, slalom, moguls,** and **half-pipe.**

As in regular skiing, the downhill snowboard does not have many turns. It is mainly a speed contest. As in slalom skiing, slalom snowboarding has plenty of turns. Just as in freestyle skiing, the moguls call for rough riding and bump jumping. The half-pipe is named for the area where it is held. The snow is molded into a channel, and the course looks like the bottom half of pipe. The contestants do stunts like skateboarders do on a ramp.

Today, more snowboarders than ever can be found on the slopes. According to the United Ski Industries Association, more than half of the snowboarders are under the age of 17.

Coca-Cola Jr. Nastar (National Standard Race)

THE NYACK LIBRARY
NYACK, N. Y. 10960

More than 100,000 kids race Nastar each year, and many race with snowboards

SNOWBOARD COMPETITIONS

In 1987 a world championship event was held in Colorado. In the 1987-88 season, more than $80,000 in prize money was offered. In 1988, the World Cup of Snowboarding began. This is a series of pro contests. Men's and women's events are held in both Europe and North America. Shredders from many countries gather together to shred the slopes. Many of the snowboard competitors belong to teams. The teams are usually sponsored by equipment makers.

Half-pipe competitions on Mt. Hood, Oregon

As in freestyle skiing, skiers can compete in either one snowboarding event or all of them. Unlike freestyle, snowboarding has many top people who participate in all four events. It cannot be said that one event is harder than another. It depends on a skier's background.

Downhill Racing

In the downhill event, there are two main goals. Contestants must gain great speed and must control their speed. It is not hard to control a board going straight down a hill, but downhill courses also have turns. Speed shredders can reach 60 or 70 miles per hour.

Snowboarding action on the turns

Dual Slalom Racing

In the **dual slalom,** two boarders try to go as fast as they can while going through side-by-side sets of poles. The poles are placed in pairs, called gates. The contestants must go through each gate without falling or missing a gate. If they miss one, they are out of the race. If they get through all the gates, they can go for pure speed. This carries them to the finish line.

Moguls

In the mogul event, shredders must have the same basic skills as freestyle skiers. They have to plan their courses and know how to get through them. As in the slalom, they want to shred as straight a line as they can. As in the freestyle, they do not want to bust the wrong bumps.

Like freestylers, mogul shredders have to be human springs. They need to absorb the shock with their legs. It is more difficult to land on a board than on skis.

Half-Pipe Contests

Many snowboarders think that the half-pipe is the most exciting event because they do not have to worry so much about time. They just try to show their best stunts. There is a time limit, however, and they can lose points if they are too slow.

Many half-pipe tricks are similar to those in surfing and skateboarding. Like a surfer, boarders can do cutbacks and quick drops. Like a skateboarder, they can do spins and jumps. They can also do them at high speed.

Most shredders think that the biggest thrill is big air. If they use their speed properly, they can pop off the walls. If they do it just right, they can get monster air. They can get as high as ten feet above the ground. Then they hang there and do some **tweakin'** for their fans. This means they grab their boards and do weird twists like the **roast beef,** the **stale fish,** or the **J-tear air.**

FOR MORE INFORMATION

Organized Competition

The freestyle section of the United States Skiing Association (USSA) offers many programs and contests. Join the USSA and you will always know what is going on.

Or write to:
> Freestyle US Skiing
> PO Box 100
> Park City, UT 84060

Age groups for young people are as follows:

Junior I	16 to 18 years old
Junior II	14 to 15 years old
Junior III	12 to 13 years old
Junior IV	10 to 11 years old
Junior V	9 years old and under

If you want to compete in snowboarding, ask a snowboarding instructor to help you. He or she will direct you to the right people.

For more information about some of the special programs for freestyle skiing and snowboarding, contact one of the following summer camp programs.

Freestyle & Snowboard Summer Camp
RD # 1 Box 2240
Kingfield, ME 04947

For ski racing, freestyle or snowboards:
Summer Ski Camp
4545 Blackcomb Way
Box 98
Whistler, B.C., Canada V0N 1B0

For ski and racing techniques:
Keystone Camp Coordinator
Box 38
Keystone, CO 80435

Ages 10 and up — freestyle training with trampolines, aerial and ballet, bungie rigs, pole flip ramp, and more, for advanced levels:
Waterville Valley Summer Camps
Box 553
Compton, NH 032223

For freestyle — ballet, moguls, and aerials with coaching by World Cup and Olympic competitors:
Freestyle International Inc.
2775 Oquirrh
Salt Lake City, UT 84108

For snowboard, half-pipe, and alpine:
High Cascade Snowboard Camp
PO Box 6622
Bend, OR 97708

For snowboarding:
U.S. Snowboard Training Center
Box 261
Brightwood, OR 97011

For snowboarding, freeriding, half-pipe, and alpine:
Mount Hood Snowboard Camp
4457 SE Wynnwood Dr
Hillsboro, OR 97120

For snowboarding, freeriding, half-pipe, and alpine:
Great Western Snowboard Camp
Box 774483
Steamboat Springs, CO 80477

For slalom, giant slalom, and Super G:
Mt. Hood Summer Ski Camp
Box 317
Government Camp, OR 97028

For freestyle, mogul, ballet, and aerial:
Great Western Freestyle Camps
Box 774483
Steamboat Springs, CO 80477

For a camp sponsored by Rossignol, with emphasis on slalom, GS, and technical skill development:
Timberline Summer Ski and Race Camp
Timberline Lodge, OR 97028

For mogul skiing:
Snowbird Mogul Skiing Programs
PO Box 920088
Snowbird, UT 84092

Hugo Bonatti of Austria skiing aerials in Albertville, France, at the 1992 Winter Olympics

Liz McIntyre (USA) skiing moguls during 1992 Winter Olympics in Albertville, France

GLOSSARY

Aerial skiing: ski routines in which the skier jumps from a ramp

Back scratcher: aerial (or mogul) jump in which the skis almost touch the skier's back

Ballet skiing: ski routines in which the skier spins, jumps, and flips on fairly flat ground

Big air: rising high above the ground on a snowboard

Downhill: speed race in skiing or snowboarding

Dual slalom: snowboard race in which two boarders attempt to slide between one of two side-by-side sets of poles placed in pairs at the same time

Gates: poles (placed in pairs) between which skiers or snowboarders attempt to slide in a slalom event

Half-pipe: snowboard event in which the contestants perform tricks in a snow channel shaped like the bottom half of a pipe

Helicopter: aerial, or mogul, jump in which the skier makes at least one complete turn

Hotdogging: performing simple ski tricks in order to simply have fun or show off

Inverted jump: aerial jump in which the skier does at least one somersault

J-tear air: jump used in the half pipe event in snowboarding competition

Moguls: sizable bumps on a ski slope

Mogul skiing: ski routines in which the skier races, demonstrates form, and jumps in a mogul field

Monster air: rising extremely high above the ground on a snowboard

Pole flip: type of ballet ski routine in which the skier pushes off with the poles and does a slow somersault

Pop: aerial, or mogul, jump in which the skier maintains a straight body position in the air

Roast beef: jump used in the half-pipe event of a snowboarding competition

THE NYACK LIBRARY
NYACK, N. Y. 10960

Road pizza: person who has taken a bad fall on a snowboard

Shredding: snowboarding

Shredder: snowboarder

Shredhead: snowboarder

Shred sled: snowboard

Slalom: skiing or snowboarding between a series of poles placed in pairs. A dual slalom is a race

Slow dog noodle: sitting back on skis and spinning very slowly

Snurfer: earliest version of the snowboard

Spread eagle: aerial, or mogul, jump in which the skier spreads the arms and legs in the air

Stale fish: jump used in the half-pipe event in a snowboarding competition

Stinkbug: snowboarding with the knees too far apart

Tweakin': doing special jumps, in which the contestant grabs the snowboard, in the half-pipe event of a snowboarding competition

Wong Banger: ballet flip in which a shoulder roll in the air is followed by a handspring

Zudnik: aerial, or mogul, jump in which the skier assumes a jackknife position

INDEX

THE NYACK LIBRARY
NYACK, N. Y. 10960